SOMEWHERE IN THE PACIFIC

Neal Bell

BROADWAY PLAY PUBLISHING INC
224 E 62nd St, NY, NY 10065
www.broadwayplaypub.com
info@broadwayplaypub.com

Cover illustration by McClelland Barclay

First published by B P P I in the collection *Plays From Playwrights Horizons, Volume 2* in 2010
This printing: June 2016
I S B N: 978-0-88145-666-0

Book design: Marie Donovan
Page make-up: Adobe InDesign
Typeface: Palatino
Printed and bound in the U S A

SOMEWHERE IN THE PACIFIC was first performed at Playwrights Horizons on 17 May 1995. The cast and creative contributors were:

HOBIE .... Adam Trese
CHOTKOWSKI .... Michael Gaston
MCGUINESS .... Silas Weir Mitchell
DUANE .... Charlie Schiff
BILLY .... Leo Marks
CAPTAIN ALBERS .... Ross Bickell
LIEUTENANT DE LUCCA .... Peter Rini
VOICE ON P A .... Ari Fliakos
JAPANESE SOLDIERS .... Ross Salinger, Ari Fliakos
INTERROGATORS........................ Ross Salinger, Ari Fliakos

Director .... Mark Brokaw
Set design consultant .... Riccardo Hernandez
Costume design .... Therese Bruck
Lighting design .... Anne M Padien
Sound design .... Michael Clark
Casting .... Janet Foster
Production manager .... Jack O'Connor
Production stage manager .... Michael Ritchie

CHARACTERS & SETTING

ALBERS, *Navy Captain, forties*
DE LUCCA, *a Navy Lieutenant,* ALBERS's *aide*
BILLY, *a Navy Seaman First Class, nineteen*
CHOTKOWSKI, *Marine, early thirties*
HOBIE, *Marine, early twenties*
DUANE, *Marine, early twenties*
McGUINESS, *Marine, early twenties*

A Liberty Ship, being used to transport troops.

Late July, 1945. Somewhere in the Pacific.

Scene One

(The foredeck of a battered Liberty Ship being used to transport troops.)

(Open water. The Central Pacific. Night)

*(Four Marines have come topside in their underwear, unable to sleep in the stifling heat below. The oldest—*CHOTKOWSKI, *thirty-one—is standing at the rail, looking out.)*

*(The others—*DUANE, *nineteen, and* MCGUINESS *and* HOBIE, *both in their mid-twenties—lie on the deck in their skivvies, smoking.)*

*(*HOBIE *looks at* CHOTKOWSKI.*)*

HOBIE: Anything?

*(*CHOTKOWSKI *doesn't respond.)*

HOBIE: Chotkowski!

CHOTKOWSKI: Dark as an ass-hole.

MCGUINESS: You should know—...

DUANE: *(Of the ocean's immensity)* Lotta miles and miles...

MCGUINESS: —spend enougha yer waking hours excavating.

DUANE: Miles and miles of miles and miles...

HOBIE: Where the *fuck* are we going? *This* time?

DUANE: The orders said Okinawa.

HOBIE: They don't need us on Okinawa.
They got the Tenth Army moppin' up.
We're going somewhere else.

CHOTKOWSKI: What else is left? The Mainland.

HOBIE: Right. They booked us into the Tokyo Hilton.

McGUINESS: That's the scuttlebutt.

HOBIE: That's what you heard? *I* heard my wife was faithful, still.

DUANE: You said your wife would spread for loose change.

HOBIE: So you get my drift.

DUANE: Your wife is a tramp?

HOBIE: The *other* drift.

DUANE: They *haven't* booked us into the Tokyo Hilton?

McGUINESS: *(To* DUANE*)* When your momma used to bounce you on her knee—did you land on your head?

*(*DUANE *gets up, joining* CHOTKOWSKI *at the rail.)*

DUANE: Miles and miles...

McGUINESS: *(Making the sound of a baby being bounced on its head)* "Bonk—bonk—bonk—bonk—"

DUANE: What my daddy'd always say, we'd be driving along, he sold vacuum cleaners, except no one could afford 'em, you know? "That's about all there is to this godforsaken, piss-poor state, just a lot of miles and miles of miles and miles..." My daddy thought that was funny.

McGUINESS: That's because I bet *his* momma dandled him badly, too. Like a family curse, musta been. It's sad: "bonk, bonk, bonk, bonk..."

*(*DUANE *points at something above the horizon.)*

DUANE: What the hell is that?

CHOTKOWSKI: *(Suddenly tenser)* Where?

DUANE: That glow out there...right over those waves... like a buncha falling stars...

CHOTKOWSKI: *(Relaxing)* Flying fish.

DUANE: Oh.

CHOTKOWSKI: You've seen 'em before.
They always amaze you.
Fucking flying fish.

DUANE: *(Peering out into the dark) Are* they fucking?

MCGUINESS: "Bonk. Bonk. Bonk. Bonk."

HOBIE: *(Bitter, almost under his breath)* The Mainland?
(Pause)
Why don't they just shoot us right now?
Get it over with?

CHOTKOWSKI: Why don't you shut the fuck up? You fucking pussy.
(Pause)
I heard something about Korea.
Maybe *that's* where we're going in.

DUANE: Korea?

MCGUINESS: That's a country, Duane. Sticks out at the Nips—like this. *(He gives* DUANE *the bird.)*

CHOTKOWSKI: We grab up all the airfields—puts us right in Japan's backyard—

HOBIE: Nobody is going to Korea.

DUANE: The *Koreans* are.

*(*MCGUINESS *makes a final "bonk".)*

(The light changes, brighter. CHOTKOWSKI *looks up.)*

CHOTKOWSKI: Break in the clouds.

DUANE: God. Look at that moon.

HOBIE: Don't that make us a target?

CHOTKOWSKI: *(Clamping down on his own nerves)* If anyone was out there.

DUANE: *(Bravado)* All I see is fucking flying fish. And this band of light like a road on the water. All the way back to the States. We're alone.

MCGUINESS: Except, Duh-wayne, it don't work like in the cartoons. You don't see a great big slanted eye looking out of a giant periscope.

(Pause, as HOBIE joins DUANE and CHOTKOWSKI, staring out at the night.)

HOBIE: Shooting gallery. Moon right there and us in front of it. Picking our butts. Let the buck-tooth bastards draw a bead on us. Blam. *(He turns to yell up at the bridge:)* ZIG-ZAG, YOU SONS-OF-BITCHES! Jesus. Fucking Navy...

(Pause. It gets darker.)

DUANE: It was just one sorry tear in the clouds. It's gone. See: dark as an asshole.

MCGUINESS: You should know.

CHOTKOWSKI: And *now*, no Jap could make us out, we're starting to zig-zag. Figures.

(A very young sailor, Seaman BILLY DUPRE, appears, taking a final bite of a banana.)

HOBIE: Fucking Navy...

(The Marines now notice the sailor.)

HOBIE: No offense there, swabbie.

BILLY: You men wanta smoke? You should go below decks.

MCGUINESS: You should suck my dick.

DUANE: It's an oven down there.

BILLY: There's a black-out, though.

MCGUINESS: Like say there *was* a pig-boat fulla demented gooks out there, you think they could glaum the glowing butt of this fucking Lucky?

BILLY: You aren't the only men on this ship.

CHOTKOWSKI: That's a fact. And that means...

BILLY: Maybe *you* guys don't die. But the rest of us do.

(Pause. CHOTKOWSKI, *with elaborate disdain, flicks his cigarette over the side.)*

BILLY: See, the rest of us—we forget where we are, for a second or two, we throw a candy-wrapper over the side, a banana peel— *(As he speaks, he tucks the banana-peel away in a pocket of his dungarees.)*

CHOTKOWSKI: *One cigarette butt,* Seaweed.

BILLY: Times how many men on this leaking tub?
—three hundred and fifty cigarette butts.
And how many "Dear John" letters do you nautical bell-hops get?
All of *them* in the drink.
We leave a trail. The Japs find us. Down we go.
But you guys don't die.

(Pause. MCGUINESS *stubs his cigarette out on the deck.)*

MCGUINESS: So Commodore, tell me—who do I ask for permission to take a dump? *(Satisfied with his dig, gets up and signals for* DUANE *to go with him.)* Duane.

DUANE: I already took a dump, McGuiness. Let me finish my smoke.

MCGUINESS: *(Pointing at* BILLY*)* O K. But some place where the air don't smell like a mackerel's heinder?

DUANE: *(Not getting it)* Don't believe I ever sniffed a mackerel up that close.

*(*MCGUINESS, *sighing, shakes his head and exits.)*

(With that heckler gone, BILLY *tries to explain himself.)*

BILLY: A buddy of mine, he was on a ship...and they think it's because *they* were leaving a wake of crap, like a giant floating arrow: "Japs! Hit this!"...

CHOTKOWSKI: Did your buddy make it? *(Pointing up)* Or is he up there?

HOBIE: "Hey you—with the wings and the harp! Put out that butt!"

BILLY: My buddy, I think, was dessert. For some well-fed shark.

(Pause)

CHOTKOWSKI: *You* seen any fighting?

BILLY: Not yet. Does that mean I can't have an opinion?

(CHOTKOWSKI stares at BILLY a moment, then starts to exit.)

CHOTKOWSKI: Pogies. Christ. *(He is gone.)*

DUANE: *(In a reverie)* Three hundred and fifty cigarette butts...

HOBIE: *(To BILLY, answering his question)* It means you don't know enough shit to *concoct* an opinion.
Fucking pogie...
(He grinds his cigarette out and exits.)

(DUANE and BILLY, left alone, look out at the dark.)

DUANE: I know you weren't talking 'bout all at once. But it *coulda* been all at once...shooting out in the dark, what a sight that'd be...three hundred and fifty falling stars...like a *school* of fucking flying fish.

BILLY: They *are* fucking, ya know.

(DUANE looks at BILLY, surprised.)

BILLY: How do you think they get up there? They start to hump way down, is what I heard. And they buck and they thrash all the way to the top, and their wings are pumping, faster and faster, and when they come—they come so hard—they go up. In the air. They just—take off...and it's like they were back in the ocean again—that dark, and deep—'till they fall back into the sky below 'em, ker-splunk, ker-splunk, ker-splunk, ker-splunk, ker-splunk: "What the *hell* was that?" But they can't figure it out. So they shrug and they keep on fugging.

(Pause. DUANE—*who's never had someone share one of his reveries—is unsettled.)*

DUANE: You been at sea too long, Jack Tar. You're going Asiatic.

BILLY: Maybe I am.

DUANE: *(Moving away from* BILLY*)* Well I need me another smoke. So I'm headin' below. Like you said.

BILLY: It's an oven. *You* said. *(Pause)* I won't tell. If you want to stay topside.

DUANE: Some other time.

BILLY: You bet. We can shoot the breeze...

*(*DUANE *shrugs, embarrassed, and exits. Hungry for contact,* BILLY *watches him go.)*

BILLY: We can shoot a few Nips.
We can shoot ourselves.
Fuck. *Fuck.* FUCK.

*(*BILLY *starts to exit, when* HOBIE *re-enters, from the opposite side.)*

HOBIE: Hey sailor.

*(*BILLY *stops.)*

HOBIE: What's your name?

BILLY: Billy.

HOBIE: Come here.

BILLY: What for?

(But BILLY, *before he can get an answer, approaches.)*

HOBIE: I haven't seen my wife in a year and a half. She don't write, anymore.
She useta...

BILLY: Why did she stop?

HOBIE: Something told her I was expendable.

(Pause)

*(*HOBIE *suddenly grabs the sailor, kissing him hard on the mouth.)*

*(*BILLY *pulls away, firm but not fighting. He stares at* HOBIE.*)*

BILLY: But you aren't. Marines are immortal. Right?

(Now BILLY *kisses* HOBIE—*first tenderly, and then more and more ferociously.)*

(The lights fade.)

Scene Two

(On the bridge. A few moments earlier. CAPTAIN ALBERS *looks out at the night, through a pair of binoculars.* LIEUTENANT DE LUCCA *eyes him with concern. Both men are wearing life-jackets.)*

DE LUCCA: Calm tonight.

ALBERS: *(Lowering the binoculars)* It's always calm.

DE LUCCA: Are you tight, sir?

(Pause. ALBERS *taps his chest.)*

ALBERS: Calm in here. Where I know things. *(Pause)* Am I *what*?

DE LUCCA: I heard about your son.

ALBERS: My son.

DE LUCCA: I'm sorry, sir.

ALBERS: Did you two ever meet?

DE LUCCA: At the Officers' Club, one time. At Pearl.
I was tight. I thought he was you.

ALBERS: I wish he was. I wish *he* was standing here...
(The light gets brighter.)

DE LUCCA: Sir?

ALBERS: Right here. Looking out at the night...feeling
the breeze...

DE LUCCA: The moon's come out.

ALBERS: Smelling the air...

DE LUCCA: Do you think we should make a course-
correction?

ALBERS: Rotten coconut-smell...what a terrible stink...
Must be a raggedy-ass little island out there. One
pathetic palm tree. One dead Jap underneath it. Big
buck-teeth in a grin... *(He takes a much-read letter out of
his pocket, unfolds it.)*

DE LUCCA: *Sir?* You did give us a standing order: if the
weather changed—while you were asleep—

ALBERS: Am I sleeping?

(DE LUCCA, hearing ALBERS's tone, looks away.)

ALBERS: What's our speed?

DE LUCCA: About seventeen knots—

ALBERS: —which is fast enough to out-run a sub, don't
you think?
If a sub should spot us. If there *is* a sub out there.
If we start to zig-zag, won't that slow us down?

DE LUCCA: Yes sir.

ALBERS: Do you want to slow down?

DE LUCCA: If the moon stays out—

ALBERS: I see one rip in the clouds. And it's mending.... Look.

DE LUCCA: I'm looking, sir. We're a target.

(Pause)

ALBERS: My son would have broken, I think.

DE LUCCA: No sir.

(ALBERS reads from the letter:)

ALBERS: "I'm afraid of the men." This is what he was writing—just before he died. "My own men. McGuiness thinks it's funny, whenever he finds a dead Jap, to stand over the wretched creature and piss in its mouth."

DE LUCCA: That got by the censors?

ALBERS: Didn't go through the mail. It was found on his body. *(He points at a stain on the letter.)* This is his blood.

(Pause)

DE LUCCA: We *are* a target, sir.

ALBERS: I know. *(To himself)* Good. *(Pause)* Good.

DE LUCCA: No sir.

ALBERS: The moonlight's almost gone.

(DE LUCCA stares at ALBERS, refusing to flinch.)

ALBERS: All right. Give the order to zig-zag.

DE LUCCA: Thank you, sir.

ALBERS: And fuck *you*, Mister De Lucca. *(He crumples the letter up.)* Now tell me not to throw this over the side.

(DE LUCCA meets ALBERS's stare.)

(ALBERS holds onto the crumpled-up letter.)

DE LUCCA: I don't think your boy would have broken, sir.

ALBERS: You thought he was me? At that club? My son was *handsome*, goddammit to hell. My son was at least a head taller. And he was young...

DE LUCCA: The light was bad. It was darker than this—

ALBERS: Give the order, Mister De Lucca.

DE LUCCA: Aye aye, sir.

(DE LUCCA *exits. The light changes, darker.* ALBERS *looks again through his binoculars.*)

(*Through the P A system,* ALBERS *hears the voice of his son.*)

VOICE ON THE P A: "I'm afraid of the men. My own men."

(ALBERS *looks around, startled.*)

VOICE ON THE P A: "McGuiness thinks it's funny, whenever he finds a dead Jap, to stand over the wretched creature and piss in its mouth. I was horrified, at first, and then ashamed. And now I'm not. I'm not anything. Now I just watch. Now it just seems like war. I'm afraid of *myself.*"

ALBERS: David? (*He looks again through his binoculars, frantically searching the dark.*)

VOICE ON THE P A: "Last night it rained till the water in the foxhole I was in was up to my knees, and one side of the trench gave way, and uncovered a young Jap soldier in the muck, who hadn't started to rot completely away, except for this hole in his skull where the brains had been..."

ALBERS: David, where are you?

VOICE ON THE P A: "...The hole filled up with water too, all the night we were there, pinned down by artillery fire...and I started to plunk little pieces of coral rock in the hole in his Nipponese head. I don't know why. To hear the sound: 'splish-splish-splish-splish...'"

(The voice fades out. The Captain suddenly stops, his binoculars trained on something.)

ALBERS: What in the name of God is that?

(DE LUCCA re-enters, on edge.)

DE LUCCA: Something out there?

ALBERS: *(Pointing)* Against the moon. Two men. Can you see them?
Floating in mid-air.
Like fairies...
Holding onto each other...

(More concerned than ever, DE LUCCA watches ALBERS.)

DE LUCCA: You should try and get some rest, sir. I've squared away the watch.

ALBERS: The boy on radar say anything was around?

DE LUCCA: We're alone. All we have to do now is stay on course. Which I think even I can manage. *(Trying to make the captain smile)* Unless you agree with my father, sir—he used to say, "Kiddo, if brains were dynamite, you couldn't blow your nose."

(ALBERS does smile.)

ALBERS: All right. I don't think I can sleep, but all right. I'll pull a little blanket-duty. Call me any time—

DE LUCCA: Aye aye.

(ALBERS starts to walk off, pauses.)

ALBERS: I want you to understand, De Lucca.

DE LUCCA: Sir?

ALBERS: I'm glad my boy is dead. He's safe. I was always afraid...

(DE LUCCA *waits for* ALBERS *to finish.*)

(ALBERS *only stands there, looking out.*)

DE LUCCA: *(Prompting)* Yes sir?

ALBERS: I was always afraid.

(ALBERS *exits.* DE LUCCA *watches him go.*)

(*The lights fade.*)

Scene Three

(*High up in the air, above the ship. Near dawn*)

(BILLY *and* HOBIE, *breathing hard, hold onto each other, hanging in space.*)

HOBIE: I can't, Jesus god, I can't breathe—

BILLY: You *are* breathing.

HOBIE: Am I?

(BILLY *tries to soothe* HOBIE, *rubbing his back.*)

(HOBIE *takes it in that he is, in fact, breathing. He starts to laugh.*)

BILLY: Shh...

(HOBIE'*s laughter slowly fades.*)

HOBIE: My old lady has this kind of...down on her lip, this golden fuzz, she hates it, says it's a goddam moustache...but it's beautiful. *She's* beautiful. *(Pause)* I never knew— I must hurt her, with my beard.

BILLY: I don't think so.

HOBIE: *(Touching* BILLY'*s face)* Sandpaper.

BILLY: Wouldn't she tell you?

HOBIE: She doesn't say a lot. Hard to know what she's thinking. Women...

BILLY: Anybody.

HOBIE: What are *you* thinking?

BILLY: I'm cold.

HOBIE: So am I.

(They hold each other closer.)

HOBIE: Do you have anybody?

BILLY: I did.

HOBIE: *(Getting it)* Oh. Your buddy on that ship?

(BILLY nods.)

BILLY: He never knew he was the one—I mean, we were kids, we just said we were fooling around...but *I* wasn't fooling. He was the one.

HOBIE: Why didn't you tell him?

BILLY: I was going to...

HOBIE: Famous last words.

BILLY: No, I think my *actual* final words—he was getting on a train, I was seeing him off, pretending I could give a damn, he's leaning out a window, like an idiot, waving good-bye..."Don't take any wooden nickels!" At the top of my lungs—he's disappearing forever— "Don't do anything I wouldn't do!"

HOBIE: Like die.

BILLY: I guess.

(Now HOBIE comforts BILLY, stroking his hair.)

(BILLY cries.)

(HOBIE nuzzles him.)

HOBIE: Fucking sandpaper.

BILLY: That's what I want.

HOBIE: No you don't. I could rub you raw.

BILLY: But that's what I want.

HOBIE: Shhh...

BILLY: Is it warmer?

HOBIE: Maybe. Sun's coming up.

BILLY: *Below* us?

(BILLY *and* HOBIE *both look down, realizing at last how high they are, way up in the air.*)

BILLY: *(Pointing down)* That's my ship?

HOBIE: Or all that blue is one *hell* of a bath-tub. And that cattle-boat down there is a toy.

BILLY: What the hell are we doing up *here*?

(HOBIE *lets go of* BILLY, *who takes a step back, in the empty air.*)

HOBIE: My guess would be—unless you can flap your arms a lot harder than I can—falling.

(*Suddenly* HOBIE *plunges out of sight, with a strangled cry.*)

(BILLY, *still floating, watches him fall, mesmerized.*)

BILLY: DON'T TAKE ANY WOODEN NICKELS! DON'T DO ANYTHING I—

(BILLY *suddenly drops like a stone, disappearing with a drawn-out scream.*)

(*The lights fade.*)

Scene Four

(*The foredeck, a few moments earlier. Near dawn*)

(CHOTKOWSKI, DUANE *and* MCGUINESS—*still in their skivvies—are asleep on blankets scattered around the deck.*)

(*Suddenly* MCGUINESS *sits up, waking out of a nightmare, with a cry.*)

CHOTKOWSKI: *(Half-asleep)* What the fuck—

McGUINESS: *(Whispering)* I heard something.

CHOTKOWSKI: *(Instantly awake)* Where?

McGUINESS: *(Wanting more company)* Duane!

DUANE: Mmmph...

McGUINESS: Duh-wayne!

(DUANE struggles awake.)

DUANE: What?

McGUINESS: Listen...

DUANE: To what? *(Pause. He hears nothing unusual.)* Betty Grable was doing deep-knee-bends. On my face. Go back to sleep.

McGUINESS: No, listen—listen!

(Far off, a couple of men are humming what sounds like the turn-of-the-century novelty-number, Under The Bamboo Tree.*)*

CHOTKOWSKI: *(Tense)* What?

DUANE: All I hear is water slapping the sides...and the engines groaning away...some pitiful S O B singing one of those stupid songs he learned at his momma's knee, just to make himself even sadder than he already is... and that soft little "fut-fut-fut", hate to break the news, but that's you guys who ate too many beans, and now you're tooting away in your sleep, like a packa old dogs...

McGUINESS: Something underneath all that...like bamboo snapping...

DUANE: This bucket is old. It's just the deck creaking.

McGUINESS: Is it?

DUANE: Miss Grable better be waiting for me— wherever I was—

CHOTKOWSKI: Back home. In a barn. On top of some woebegone sheep. With fuzzy gams.

DUANE: *(Ignoring* CHOTKOWSKI*)* —if you wouldn't mind shutting the noise... *(He quickly sinks back into sleep.)*

*(*CHOTKOWSKI *stands and fakes a casual stretch.)*

MCGUINESS: *(Fighting panic)* Where the fuck are *you* going?

CHOTKOWSKI: To take a leak. You wanta help me aim?

MCGUINESS: Go to hell.

CHOTKOWSKI: *(Starting to exit)* There is nobody out there, Mac.

MCGUINESS: Then why are you running?

CHOTKOWSKI: *(Unexpectedly serious)* Because I'm scared. I'm shitless. I ran, before. Didn't you go with me? Over that hill? *(Pause)* See you in the movies, friend.

*(*CHOTKOWSKI *hurriedly exits, leaving* MCGUINESS *alone with the sleeping* DUANE.*)*

(The offstage humming has turned into singing, nearer. The words are finally clear, and the voices seem to be two men who are substituting "R"s for "L"s in the song.)

VOICES: *(Offstage, to the tune of* Under The Bamboo Tree*)* If you *r*ak-a-me, *r*ike I *r*ak-a-you and we *r*ak-a both the same...

MCGUINESS: *(Whispering over the singing)* Someone *is* out there. "*R*ike I *r*ike-a you"? Oh Jesus—Duane?

(But DUANE *sleeps on, and the voices continue singing, underneath* MCGUINESS *babbling on in his panic:)*

VOICES: *(Offstage)* ...I *r*ak-a-say, this very day, I *r*ak-a-change your name...

McGUINESS: *(Over the singing)* Duane? These bastards never learned this bull-fucking-shit at a *white* woman's knee—they can't say "L". They can't say "L"! Duane!

(DUANE doesn't stir, as two men stealthily enter, singing—dressed as Japanese soldiers, wearing cartoon-masks of the evil "yellow peril" of American propaganda—exaggerated slanted eyes buck-teeth, and mustard-colored skin.)

(McGUINESS watches, paralyzed with terror, as one of the soldiers—attaching his bayonet to his rifle—approaches him.)

(The other tip-toes up to Duane, brandishing a huge and gleaming machete.)

(The soldiers sing, as they stalk their prey:)

SOLDIERS: ...'Cause I *r*ove-a you and *r*ove-a you true and if you-a *r*ove-a-me,
one *r*ive as two, two *r*ive as one, under the bamboo tree.

(On the word "tree", the "Japanese" SOLDIERS attack. One bayonets McGUINESS in the chest. The other, with his machete, hacks away at something in DUANE's boxer-shorts.)

(DUANE screams and then—in shock—passes out. The SOLDIER, with his free hand, pulls a bloody peeled banana out of DUANE's boxers.)

(He holds the severed banana up to show his comrade, who nods at the trophy. McGUINESS, mortally wounded, watches in horror.)

McGUINESS: *(To the SOLDIER)* You cut it off??

(The SOLDIER stuffs the bloody banana in DUANE's open mouth.)

McGUINESS: No!

(Now both of the SOLDIERS start to retreat, singing again:)

SOLDIERS: 'Cause I *rove*-a you, and *rove*-a you true and
if you-a *rove*-a me, one *rive* as two, two *rive* as one,
under the bamboo tree.

(The SOLDIERS *are gone. The bloody banana still protrudes
from* DUANE'*s mouth.)*

MCGUINESS: Duane? *(He tries to crawl to his fallen
comrade. But he's lost his strength and collapses, halfway
there.)*

*(*DUANE, *on his back, not moving, starts to chew the banana
stuck in his mouth.)*

*(*MCGUINESS, *appalled, keeps watching as the banana
disappears.)*

(When it's gone, DUANE *lies still again.)*

MCGUINESS: Duane? ...Are you dead?

*(*DUANE *doesn't respond.)*

MCGUINESS: Are you dead *now*?

*(*DUANE *seems to be.)*

MCGUINESS: That time in the valley? When Chotkowski
and I were lost? Remember? I never told you this...I
was going to, I swear to god...I ran away. I wasn't lost.
I ran like hell. I thought we all had. I thought you were
right behind me.

*(*MCGUINESS *is chilled as* DUANE *unsteadily starts to sit
up.)*

MCGUINESS: The way all the leaves were shaking? You
figured a wind had come up. Except it was shrapnel.
Ripping through that wall of green and Chotkowski
started stumbling back, like he'd heard something *I*
didn't hear—maybe one goddam C O with a brain in
his head yelling, "Get the fuck out!" ...So I ran... And I
thought you were right behind me. You son-of-a-bitch.

(DUANE *is now on all fours, staring balefully at* McGUINESS.)

McGUINESS: I went back for you. I tried. And then I *did* get lost, I fell into a river, I cut myself to shit on that razor-grass, you remember what I looked like, when I finally stumbled into the camp? And you helped me burn the leeches off?

(DUANE, *locking eyes with his buddy, vomits up the banana, all over his blanket.*)

(McGUINESS *has to look away.*)

McGUINESS: You believed me then. Why can't you believe me now?

DUANE: Because I'm dead. And I know things. (*He thumps his chest.*) Here. In my heart.

McGUINESS: I loved you, you son-of-a-bitch. Like my own brother.

DUANE: I'm dead.

(DUANE *stands and exits, pulling behind him the vomit-covered blanket.* McGUINESS *watches him go.*)

McGUINESS: I LEFT YOU BEHIND!
DUANE!
BUT I WENT BACK FOR YOU!
I WENT BACK!

(CHOTKOWSKI *re-enters, casual, and lies back down on the deck, where he was sleeping.*)

(*As he and* McGUINESS *bicker,* DUANE *re-enters, unnoticed—with an unsoiled blanket—and also settles down to sleep.*)

CHOTKOWSKI: (*Looking up at the sky*) The Southern Cross is gone—

McGUINESS: Where the fuck have *you* been?

CHOTKOWSKI: I was taking a leak. Did you want to help me aim?

MCGUINESS: They were *here*!

CHOTKOWSKI: Who?

MCGUINESS: Who the hell are we fighting? The Japs! They got Duane!

CHOTKOWSKI: You were dreaming, buddy. Duane is snoring his head off, right beside you.

(MCGUINESS *looks over, stunned to see that* DUANE *is back, intact.*)

CHOTKOWSKI: And it looks to me, from the way his skivvies are standin' up and salutin'—Miss Grable musta renewed her labors. "*One*-two, *back* straight, *knees* bent..."

(MCGUINESS *gives* DUANE *a nudge.*)

MCGUINESS: Duane?

DUANE: *(Asleep)* Glumsh...

MCGUINESS: *(Nudging harder)* Duane!

DUANE: *What?* What the Sam-goddam-Hill do you want?

MCGUINESS: *(Reassured, finally breathing again)* Nothing.

CHOTKOWSKI: Bucking for a Section Eight.

DUANE: Shoot a toe off, then. In the morning. Geez... *(He drifts off.)*

MCGUINESS: Henry?

CHOTKOWSKI: Would you stop beating your gums?

MCGUINESS: In the valley...

CHOTKOWSKI: We aren't *in* the valley, now.

MCGUINESS: But won't there be valleys in Japan?

(CHOTKOWSKI *doesn't answer.*)

McGUINESS: Why did you run?

CHOTKOWSKI: Are you writing a book? I just did. So did half the platoon. It don't keep me up nights.

McGUINESS: Then why aren't you asleep?

(CHOTKOWSKI *rolls away from* McGUINESS.)

(*Offstage, nearby, we hear what sounds like a body falling onto the deck from a very great height. Then another*)

McGUINESS: Chotkowski! What the fuck was that?

(CHOTKOWSKI *snores.* DUANE *does too.*)

(McGUINESS, *alone and upset, looks out at the night.*)

McGUINESS: Somebody just came on board...

(*The lights fade.*)

Scene Five

(*A moment earlier. Amidships. Dawn*)

(*The stage is empty.*)

(*Suddenly* HOBIE *drops from out of the sky, hitting the deck with a thud. Though he lands on his feet, and he isn't hurt, he's shaken up.*)

(HOBIE *looks around him, trying to get his bearings.*)

HOBIE: What the...

(*A second later,* BILLY *hits the deck, a few feet away. He's rattled too, but also unhurt from the fall.*)

(*Seeing* BILLY, *everything comes back in a rush to* HOBIE.)

HOBIE: Oh. (*He doesn't like what he remembers.*) Oh Christ... (*Embarrassed, he gets a cigarette out, lights up.*)

(BILLY *doesn't catch on to* HOBIE's *mood.*)

BILLY: Are you all right?

HOBIE: Extremely swell, I think. Yourself?

BILLY: Not bad.

HOBIE: Good enough. So I'll see you in Tokyo, maybe...

(Now BILLY *gets it. He's hurt, but he tries not to show it.)*

BILLY: *(Trying to kid)* Not if I see you first.

*(*HOBIE *snorts and starts to exit, stops. Some left-over tenderness makes him want to leave* BILLY *with something.)*

HOBIE: *(Holding up his cigarette)* The only dirty joke my wife ever told me: "Do you smoke after sex?" "I don't know—I never looked."

(Pause)

BILLY: What color is her hair? Your wife.

HOBIE: How the hell should I know? *(As if he'd never said this before)* I haven't seen my wife in a year and a half. She don't write anymore. She useta...

BILLY: Why did she stop?

*(*McGUINESS—*edgy, looking around for the source of the ominous thuds he heard in the previous scene—appears. He stops when he sees the two men talking.)*

(The tension between BILLY *and* HOBIE *is so clear that* McGUINESS *hides and listens in.)*

HOBIE: I sent her a letter, I told her to stuff a piece of paper down her pants, let it stew all day, and then scribble a note on that. And she did. And it worked. I could smell her...a couple of days...

BILLY: And?

HOBIE: That's all she wrote.

BILLY: Why?

HOBIE: Because women know everything. Don't they? How far you'll ever get in your life, who you're screwing, who you'd *like* to screw but you never will, how much more you drank last night than you said,

what you *really* think about the way her chin is starting
to double up, how you hate the little sounds she makes
when you're drilling her— "yip, yip, yip" ...how to cut
her losses...

BILLY: She hasn't lost you.

HOBIE: Yet. Fuck you.

BILLY: You just did.

HOBIE: What the hell are you talking about.

BILLY: I can smell you on my hands.

(Pause. HOBIE *comes back to* BILLY, *getting up into his
face.)*

HOBIE: Do I smell like a body?

BILLY: I like the way a man—

HOBIE: Do I smell like a body washing up on a beach?
I am going to die. Next week. Maybe sooner. My wife
knows that. Why the hell don't you? You *also* yip like
a goddam dog when you come. But my wife is a lot
better fuck. So you lose. *(He grabs* BILLY.*)* If you *ever* try
to buck me up again, you son-of-a-bitch...I will beat
you to a bloody pulp. And nobody will stop me. No
one. I'll say you put your hand on my dick.

BILLY: And you won't be lying. Will you?

*(*HOBIE *pulls* BILLY *so close, they could kiss. But they don't.)*

HOBIE: You won't be recognizable. I'll heave you over.
You can wash up on a beach.

BILLY: Beside you? How would that look? In the
shallows...bumping against you... *(Making the sound of
surf)* Poooosh...poooosh...I don't even like you. I don't
even know your name.

(Pause. HOBIE *pushes* BILLY *away and exits, trying not to
run.)*

(BILLY *grabs a mop that's lying around, and starts—a little frantically—to mop the deck.*)

BILLY: Rub it raw...rub it harder...HARDER...make it bleed...

(MCGUINESS *steps out of his hiding-place.*)

MCGUINESS: Hey sailor...

(BILLY *stares at* MCGUINESS *as the lights fade.*)

Scene Six

(*The officers' wardroom—set up like a cop's investigation-room, with a metal chair in a pool of light.*)

(CHOTKOWSKI *sits in the glare, pissed off and holding a piece of paper.*)

(*Behind him, in the shadows, are* DE LUCCA *and* ALBERS.)

DE LUCCA: (*Offering*) Cuppa joe?

CHOTKOWSKI: The way you swab-jockies make it?

DE LUCCA: O K. (*Reading from a list, to the Captain*) This is Corporal Henry Chotkowski. Gunner. Fifth Division.

CHOTKOWSKI: Anybody care to tell me what the fuck this is all about?

ALBERS: Would you read the letter, Corporal?

CHOTKOWSKI: (*Of the paper in his hand*) This snivelling shit? I read it.

ALBERS: Out loud. In your normal tone of voice.

CHOTKOWSKI: Look, Captain, I don't want to be in the show—

ALBERS: This is not an audition.

CHOTKOWSKI: —wear a coconut bra, that crap—

ALBERS: Did you hear me, corporal?

CHOTKOWSKI: Maybe it's good for morale, but myself, I would rather indulge in a little Acey-Deucey. Or take a big dump. Or jag off.

(Pause)

ALBERS: *(Steely)* Read the letter.

(Pause. CHOTKOWSKI *starts to read.)*

CHOTKOWSKI: "Dear Dad—"

ALBERS: Skip down a few paragraphs. "The hole filled up..."

CHOTKOWSKI: I seen a lot worse than this—

ALBERS: So have I. Would you read.

CHOTKOWSKI: *(Reading)* "The hole filled up with water too, all the night we were there, pinned down by artillery fire...and I started to plunk little pieces of coral rock in the hole in his Nipponese head. I don't know why. To hear the sound: `splish—...'"

ALBERS: *(Interrupting)* That's enough. *(To* DE LUCCA*)* He's not the one. Bring the next man in.

*(*DE LUCCA *exits.)*

(Pause. CHOTKOWSKI *looks like there's more he'd like to say.)*

ALBERS: Thank you, corporal. That'll be all.

*(*CHOTKOWSKI *starts to leave, then hesitates.)*

CHOTKOWSKI: Sir...

ALBERS: *(Answering the unasked question)* If I knew, I couldn't tell you. We rendezvous with the fleet at Ie Shima, off Okinawa. You men get your orders there.

CHOTKOWSKI: They don't need us at Okinawa.

ALBERS: Then you go wherever they tell you to. So do I.

Why, Corporal?
Are you afraid?

(Pause)

CHOTKOWSKI: Aren't you?

ALBERS: No. Not anymore.

CHOTKOWSKI: Then you're a fool, sir.

ALBERS: Come again?

CHOTKOWSKI: You're a goddam fool.

ALBERS: I see. Is that your ticket out? To get slapped in the brig? You can stand at a porthole, I'll give you my own field glasses? You can watch your buddies die on the beach...without you?

(CHOTKOWSKI trembles with fury.)

ALBERS: Dismissed.

(CHOTKOWSKI can't even move, he's so angry.)

ALBERS: *(Yelling)* Mister De Lucca!
Send the next one in.
(To CHOTKOWSKI, as he plucks the letter from the corporal's hand:) Somebody read this over the P A. Trying to make me break. I would like to know who. I remember the voice. Would you get the hell out of my wardroom?

(Speechless, CHOTKOWSKI spins around and thunders out, as the lights fade.)

Scene Seven

(Amidships. A few moments earlier)

(BILLY stares at MCGUINESS, who's grinning at him.)

MCGUINESS: *(Repeating his call)* Hey sailor...

BILLY: What?

MCGUINESS: Suck my dick. *(Pause)* Suck *my* dick.

(Pause)

BILLY: Do you have one? *(He starts swabbing the deck again.)*

*(*MCGUINESS' *smile begins to congeal.)*

DE LUCCA: *(Off, voice on P A)* McGuiness! Front and center! Private McGuiness!

*(*MCGUINESS, *aggravated, looks off—not wanting to stop the game he's playing with* BILLY*.)*

MCGUINESS: Does the Captain know you're a pansy?

*(*BILLY *stops.)*

BILLY: Tell him.

(Pause)

MCGUINESS: Look: just suck my big fat dick.

DE LUCCA: *(Off, voice on P A)* McGuiness! Private Brian McGuiness!

(Pause)

BILLY: I'm off-duty in a couple of hours.
Come to the number-five turret.
It's dark enough. Has a mattress somebody dragged in there a long time ago.
It smells like a sacka dead rabbits.
Like you. It smells like you.
But it's safe. You can hear if anyone's coming. *(Pause)*

I was always afraid I would meet a man like you.
I used to have a dream...

MCGUINESS: I read somewhere that dreams are wishes. *Reader's Digest.* How 'bout that? *(He exits.)*

BILLY: In the dream, I kill the man.
I beat him to a bloody pulp.
And nobody stops me. *(He keeps swabbing the deck.)*

(The lights fade.)

Scene Eight

(The wardroom. A few moments earlier)

(DUANE is in the chair, in the pool of light.)

(Again DE LUCCA and ALBERS stand in the shadows, listening.)

(DUANE is reading from the letter.)

DUANE: *(Mid-way through)* "...except for this hole in his skull where the brains had been..." *(He starts to cry.)*

DE LUCCA: *(To ALBERS)* Is he the one you heard?

ALBERS: *(Shaking his head)* I don't know why he's crying. Son?

DUANE: I'm sorry, sir.

ALBERS: Want to talk about it?

DUANE: No, sir.

(Pause. DE LUCCA exits, to call the next man.)

ALBERS: *(Taking the letter from DUANE)* Have you been here?

DUANE: Where? *(Pause)* ...I was covered with maggots, once... This mortar hit a mass grave—...

ALBERS: Go on...

DUANE: Well, we didn't *know* that's what it was—just ahead of where we had dug in, and it all went up— WHOOOMP!—and then it was raining down on us for it seemed like hours, and we still hadn't figured out what it was, just mud and rock, we thought, but it was flesh and bone, fucking Japanese flesh and bone, coming showering down, and my buddy McGuiness— he was brushing me off, kinda hard, and he said, "Duh-wayne, don't open your eyes, not yet", but I did, I looked down, and I was, everything was moving, maggots were crawling all over me...from my helmet down to my boon-dockers. On my hands and up my nose and in my mouth. And in my mouth, and in my... Like I was dead. *(Pause)* I want to go home.

ALBERS: We all do, son.

(DE LUCCA re-enters, quietly.)

ALBERS: Your buddy's name was McGuiness?

DUANE: Yes sir.

ALBERS: Is he still with you?

DE LUCCA: Right outside.

ALBERS: Then that'll be all, Private Owensby.

DUANE: Sir? Can I ask? What happened to the man who wrote this letter?

ALBERS: He's stateside, now. On leave. With his wife. I imagine—what time is it now in San Francisco?

DE LUCCA: After noon.

ALBERS: I imagine he's still in the rack. With his better half.

DUANE: I hope so, sir.

ALBERS: Are *you* married, Private Owensby?

DUANE: I have a girl. But she sleeps around.

ALBERS: And you don't mind?

DUANE: *I* sleep around. So fair is fair.

ALBERS: You're a very modern man, Private Owensby.

DUANE: *(Not sure this is a compliment)* Thank you, sir. *(He salutes and exits.)*

(ALBERS turns to DE LUCCA.)

DE LUCCA: It was kind of you to lie.

ALBERS: You think so? Or do you honest-to-God believe I am soft and old and my brains are turning to sawdust?

(Pause)

DE LUCCA: I *don't* think you heard what you thought you did. I don't think there was anyone on the P A. What you read was just bouncing around in your bean. Having all the men on the ship take a look at this letter...

ALBERS: *Everyone* will see the sawdust. Leaking out my ears...

DE LUCCA: No, everyone will react like this poor kid. And the tougher ones will hide it better...but all of them will think about dying. Soon. On a Japanese beach. Do you need to remind them?

(Pause)

ALBERS: Call in this fellow McGuiness. End it right there. And then I will let my son rest. In a box full of maggots.

(Pause)

DE LUCCA: It isn't likely that this is the same McGuiness...

ALBERS: I hope not, Lieutenant. I pray to God not.

*(*DE LUCCA *exits.)*

*(*ALBERS *stares at the letter.)*

(The voice of ALBERS' *son comes over the P A again.)*

VOICE ON P A: "...my own men. McGuiness thinks it's funny, whenever he finds a dead Jap, to stand over the wretched creature—"

*(*ALBERS *suddenly throws his coffee-mug at the [offstage] squawk-box. We hear an explosion of static, and then complete silence.)*

(As ALBERS, *breathing heavily, looks around him, the lights fade.)*

Scene Nine

*(The galley. Later that day. BILLY's peeling potatoes,
dumping the ones he's peeled in a big pot of water.)*

*(HOBIE comes in—in his hands a "bra" made of coconut
shells, and a fake grass skirt.)*

HOBIE: What the fuck is this?

BILLY: I'm in the show tonight.

HOBIE: In a pair of coconut hooters?

BILLY: I get a few laughs.

HOBIE: Or snickers?

BILLY: What does it matter to you?

(HOBIE throws the costume down on the deck.)

HOBIE: You could just wear a sign: "I'M A POGIE."

BILLY: And what would *your* sign say?

(Pause)

HOBIE: "I'M A MORON." Great big letters. I *am* a
moron, swear to god. You can ask my wife.

(BILLY, not rising to the bait, won't enter the conversation.)

HOBIE: I don't know why she married me.
I reminded her of her father, maybe.
He was a moron—Jesus... *(Pause)* You're wasting a hell
of a lot of potato.

BILLY: Call the quartermaster.

HOBIE: Let me.

*(HOBIE takes the paring knife from BILLY. As their hands
touch, BILLY blushes and turns away, bending down to pick
up the bra and skirt.)*

BILLY: *(Of his costume)* You went through my locker?

HOBIE: Who are you? That's all. I wanted to know.

BILLY: Why?

(HOBIE, *unable to answer, keeps peeling potatoes.* BILLY *feels an urge to get away.)*

BILLY: I'm gonna be late for rehearsal... *(He starts to put on the coconut "bra" and grass skirt.)*

HOBIE: *(To keep him from going)* What was your buddy's name?

BILLY: Johnny.

HOBIE: Johnny What?

BILLY: I don't remember. Johnny the Dead Guy.

HOBIE: Do I look like him?

BILLY: I guess. In the dark. *(He's got the hula-outfit on by now.)* Do I look like your wife?

HOBIE: *(An uneasy joke)* In that get-up? You could be her twin.

BILLY: *(Of the costume)* She's a native?

HOBIE: Of Indianapolis.

(Pause. Despite himself, there's something BILLY *has to ask.)*

BILLY: You told me she was a better lay. Than me. So what does she do?

HOBIE: What does she do? It's been a long time...
She starts off in the shower. Singing.
Sounds like a cat being swung by the tail.

BILLY: I can sing better than that.

HOBIE: So can I. I say, "Drive it in the hangar, doll, and turn the motor off, for crissakes".
She can't hear me over her yowling, though.
So I have to shut her up.

BILLY: How?

HOBIE: I get into the shower *with* her.
I stick a finger inside her....

And she's already wet.
She told me one time, just the sound of my voice...

BILLY: Saying what? What you said to me? "I'll beat
you to a bloody pulp."

(Pause)

HOBIE: I'm sorry.

BILLY: Sorry? Or horny?

HOBIE: Both?

(BILLY starts to exit. HOBIE grabs him.)

HOBIE: That was a joke.

BILLY: No it wasn't.

*(HOBIE stares at BILLY, letting him go but still wanting to
touch him.)*

HOBIE: No. It wasn't.

*(Pulled by the tension between them, the two men move
closer, almost embracing.)*

*(At that moment CHOTKOWSKI enters, still angry at the
grilling he got. He stops short, seeing the men about to kiss.)*

CHOTKOWSKI: At ease, ladies.

(BILLY and HOBIE, caught by surprise, jump apart.)

HOBIE: This is not—Jesus Christ—this is not...

CHOTKOWSKI: Oh? The way it looks? It never is.

BILLY: We were rehearsing.

*(Both embarrassed and frightened by CHOTKOWSKI, BILLY
quietly starts to slip out of his "bra" and skirt.)*

CHOTKOWSKI: You coulda fooled me. *(To HOBIE)* I
thought you had found you a Navy pussy-mouth.
Get him down on his knees. Get your rocks off. More
power to you.

HOBIE: You don't care?

CHOTKOWSKI: What you do with your dick is your business, Hobart. Long as you cover my ass when we hit the beach. Maybe "cover my ass" is the wrong way of putting it. Given that gleam in your eye.

HOBIE: Fuck you.

CHOTKOWSKI: No I think I will wait for the genuine article, thanks. *(To* BILLY*)* Any room in your show for *another* novelty number?

BILLY: *(Shaking his head)* We do it up top, at the end of the day...and we only have till the light fades out...

CHOTKOWSKI: *(Ignoring)* 'Cause I got me a sorta impression I thought I would try. Of a man pinned down in a foxhole...right next to some Nipponese carcass... *(To* BILLY*)* Your Captain don't seem to understand—you stare at a mangled body too long, and you have to go this way or that: either, "that could be me, with the hole in my skull, and the rainwater filling it up" —which'll give you the horrors, I know— or "that wasn't *ever* a man like me. That has never been anything else but a chunka the landscape. Target practice". So... *(He picks up a load of potatoes.)* "A man pinned down in a foxhole, with a dead body, passing the time..." And you have to imagine that pot is a dead Jap's skull...and these spuds are rocks...Goes something like this... *(He starts to lob the potatoes into the pot of water.)*

(Each hits with an audible splash.)

*(*CHOTKOWSKI *takes his time, to make his point: splash... splash...splash...'til he's out of ammo.)*

CHOTKOWSKI: I think you two should fuck each other's brains out. While you still got 'em—dicks, brains, arms, legs, faces...

(He gets some more potatoes and starts to toss them: splash... splash...splash...splash...)

(With the kind of desperate urgency CHOTKOWSKI's *talking about,* BILLY *and* HOBIE *suddenly grab each other, in an embrace that sinks them down to the deck.)*

*(*CHOTKOWSKI *watches them, continuing to dunk potatoes: splash...splash...*
splash...)

(The lights fade.)

Scene Ten

(The wardroom. A few moments earlier)

*(*MCGUINESS *is in the chair, in the pool of light.)*

*(*ALBERS *and* DE LUCCA *stand nearby.)*

ALBERS: So you *did* know my son.

MCGUINESS: Rusty Albers?

ALBERS: *(Correcting)* David.

MCGUINESS: We called him "Rusty". You know— because of his hair. Sure...he saved my ass one night, I was staggering back to the camp, I was tight as a tick from some jungle-juice the men had been cooking up on the beach... What happens is, I get to the sentry, this two-bit Patton wants to hear the password, and—it's "lullaby"...which is so far gone from my pickled brain that I couldn't have said "lullaby" any better than fucking Hirohito could...and this by-the-book little bastard's really going to shoot!, he is drawing a bead on my virginal chest—and then Rusty—David—he's walking the line that night, he sees what's up, he tells the sentry to hold his fire, he knows me, useta sing me to sleep when I was a lad, and now don't I remember?—he's winking at me and I finally get it, I say to the sentry: "LULLABY! —motherfucker!" I tried to thank your son, the next day, he just told me not to drink so much. Or write the password down on me, some place I couldn't miss it. Like my asshole, he said, where I seemed to have wedged my head.

ALBERS: Did David talk like that?

McGUINESS: Sure he did. He was one of the guys. That's why we all liked him.

ALBERS: You know he died.

McGUINESS: Yes sir...see, we'd lost so many men by then, I was transferred out of Rusty's company—'cause there *was* no company, anymore—I was posted to the buncha gorillas I'm sharing a cage with now...I guess Rusty was on his way to Iwo Jima...

ALBERS: That's right.

McGUINESS: I'm sorry for your troubles, sir.

ALBERS: Thank you, McGuiness.

McGUINESS: And I ended up on his old man's ship. Small fucking world.

ALBERS: War seems to make strange bedfellows.

McGUINESS: That it does, sir. The strangest.

(ALBERS *hands* McGUINESS *the letter.*)

ALBERS: Have you see this letter?

McGUINESS: *(Puzzled)* Sir?

ALBERS: It was sent to me...a few weeks after David was killed. It's *from* David—Rusty...

McGUINESS: To you?

(ALBERS *nods.* McGUINESS *offers the letter back.*)

McGUINESS: Then it's gotta be private?

ALBERS: *(Taking the letter)* Didn't you hear it this morning? Booming over the squawk-box?

McGUINESS: You read it out loud?

ALBERS: No, I didn't.
Someone did. Would you like to hear it?

DE LUCCA: *(More and more alarmed)* Captain... *(Of*
MCGUINESS:*) Was* it this man's voice you heard?

ALBERS: I don't believe it was.

DE LUCCA: Then—let him go.

ALBERS: I won't keep you, young man. But listen
to this... *(Reading from the letter)* David writes, "I'm
afraid—"

MCGUINESS: You would never have guessed that, sir.

(ALBERS *gives him a look that shuts him up, and hands him
the letter again.)*

ALBERS: *You* read.

(MCGUINESS, *sensing big trouble, starts to read.)*

MCGUINESS: "I'm afraid of the men. My own men.
McGuiness thinks it's funny, whenever he finds a dead
Jap, to stand over the wretched creature and piss in its
mouth."

(ALBERS *stares at* MCGUINESS. MCGUINESS *looks at his
boots. No one speaks.)*

ALBERS: I believe it continues...

MCGUINESS: *(Reading)* "I was horrified, at first, and
then ashamed. And now I'm not. I'm not anything.
Now I just watch. Now it just seems like war. I'm
afraid of *myself.*"

(A very uncomfortable silence)

DE LUCCA: Sir?

ALBERS: *(To* DE LUCCA*)* I want you to wait for me in
your quarters.

DE LUCCA: But sir—

ALBERS: That's an order, Mister.

(DE LUCCA *reluctantly exits.*)

(ALBERS *stares at* MCGUINESS.)

ALBERS: Do you know how David died?

MCGUINESS: He was shot—

ALBERS: He shot himself. With his service revolver.
One round to the head.

(DE LUCCA *silently comes back in, unseen. He's afraid for the captain.*)

ALBERS: The commanding officer tried to cover it up.
To spare my feelings. But David was behind the lines—
so how could a Jap have gotten that close?
There were powder burns on the skin around the
entrance hole... (*Listening to the sound of the words*)
Entrance hole...exit hole... (*Pause. He suddenly screams
at* MCGUINESS.) YOU PISSED IN A DEAD MAN'S
MOUTH?

(MCGUINESS *twitches, mortified.*)

(*Suddenly* ALBERS *hauls off and slaps him, hard, in the
face.*)

(MCGUINESS *doesn't try to get away.*)

(DE LUCCA *steps forward, making his presence known. But*
ALBERS *ignores him.*)

ALBERS: My son lay where he fell, on that jungle path,
for a day and a night.... There was serious sniper-fire,
I'm told...so they couldn't recover his body. Not for a
day and a night...and I wonder if, during that night,
in the jungle—and *nothing* is darker than night in a
jungle...a Jap stepped out from behind a tree, in the
dark, and unbuttoned his fly, and pissed on my son.
All over my dead son. *Pissed* on him.

(*Again without warning,* ALBERS *slaps* MCGUINESS.)

DE LUCCA: Sir...

ALBERS: *(To* DE LUCCA*)* Would you like to spend a few days in hack? I told you to stay in your cabin.

*(*DE LUCCA *says nothing.)*

*(*MCGUINESS *starts to grin, though his mouth is bloody.)*

MCGUINESS: You know what the Japs do. Cut our dicks off.
Stuff them in our mouths.

*(*ALBERS *slaps* MCGUINESS *again.* MCGUINESS *spits some blood and smiles.)*

ALBERS: Good for you. Don't break.

MCGUINESS: I won't. I don't make any friends. So nobody can hurt me. All I can do is die. *(Pause)*
Your son had a buddy.
And his buddy blew up. He stepped on a mine.
Right next to Rusty. *David.* This bright red haze. We inhaled him. *(Pause)* Rusty cried a long time. We all knew what that meant. So we let him be. Maybe we shouldn't have. Maybe he shouldn't have been alone so much. *(He puts a finger to his head, like a gun.)* Pow...

(Pause)

ALBERS: Are you saying my son was a faggot?

*(*MCGUINESS *smiles.)*

ALBERS: My son has a wife. And a baby on the way.

MCGUINESS: Then let's hope the kid is his father's spitting image.

*(*ALBERS *hits* MCGUINESS *a final time.)*

DE LUCCA: Don't hit this man again. Sir.

ALBERS: No. I won't.

(Pause)

MCGUINESS: I didn't get that you *minded* homos.

ALBERS: What the hell are you talking about.

McGuiness: On this ship. There are *clouds* of fairies.

(Pause)

Albers: Name one.

McGuiness: Billy. Billy Somebody. He asked me to
meet him tonight. By the number-five gun.

Albers: I don't believe you.

McGuiness: Come and watch, if you want.
Hang around. Till he puts his hand on my dick.
Then arrest him.
Or let him go.
Let him jerk me off.
Nothing wrong with that.
Now, pissing on the enemy...*that's* a court-martial.
Am I right?
Or am I right?

(McGuiness smiles again—a bloody smile—at Albers.)

(The lights fade.)

Scene Eleven

(Beside a gun-turret. Night)

*(Billy waits for McGuiness. He's gripping a heavy metal
stanchion, beating a rhythm out on the palm of his other
hand.)*

*(McGuiness, in fatigues and T-shirt, sneaks up and speaks
to him from the shadows.)*

McGuiness: You signalling? To the enemy?

Billy: *(Turning, oddly calm)* Which enemy?

(McGuiness looks out.)

McGuiness: *(With total certainty)* There is somebody
out there.

BILLY: *(Looking out)* Nothing. Dark as an asshole.

McGUINESS: You should know.

(All this time, BILLY's kept the percussion up, on his palm, with the metal bar.)

McGUINESS: So what's the ditty, Mister Krupa?

BILLY: You don't recognize it? No.
Why should you? *(He sings, in rhythm to his thumping:)*
"Eternal Father, strong to save,
Whose arm hath bound the restless wave..."

(Something about BILLY's manner is making McGUINESS uneasy.)

McGUINESS: Hot below.

BILLY: Like sleeping in an oven. They say.
Not that I've ever slept in an oven.
Have you?
Sometimes it felt like an oven—my own body, when I was fucking.
I'd wake up, and the man would be gone...like I'd burned him up and he'd blown away...

McGUINESS: Take your clothes off.

(BILLY stares but doesn't move.)

McGUINESS: Come on. Hot night, two lonely guys... *(He moves closer, stepping out of the shadows.)*

BILLY: What happened to your face?

McGUINESS: You should see the other guy.

BILLY: I just want to see you.

McGUINESS: Propeller-wash. You are humping your way through the whole duty-roster.

BILLY: Trying to find somebody.

McGUINESS: Who?

(MCGUINESS *is getting too close to something. The mood
begins to evaporate.* MCGUINESS *tries to pull* BILLY *back by
singing to him.*)

MCGUINESS: "Oh hear us when we cry to Thee—"

BILLY: *(Surprised that he knows the hymn)* I thought—

MCGUINESS: You were a Cub Scout. I was a choir-boy.
We *all* had lives. *(Singing again)* "—for those in peril on
the sea."

(Pause. MCGUINESS's *got* BILLY *back, for a moment.)*

BILLY: Who hit you?

MCGUINESS: The Captain.

BILLY: Why?

MCGUINESS: Because he can.

(Pause)

BILLY: They don't lay a finger on us, faggots they catch
in the act.
They don't have to.
But they make you strip,
in front of them—
then you stand there,
with this hot light shining down and your arms at your
side,
you can't cover yourself,
and they ask you, over and over,
"Why the hell did you ever enlist?"

MCGUINESS: Bullshit. That's a campfire story.
That's you nellies trying to scare yourselves.

BILLY: One guy I heard about,
he was so afraid, he pissed himself.
And he had to keep standing there.
Arms at his side. Naked.
In the puddle.

(Pause)

McGUINESS: And then what happened?
Nothing—right?
They kicked him out.
He was free.

BILLY: Except—it said, "Sexual psychopath,"
right there on his discharge papers.
He could never get a decent job.
He could never go home.
He's still standing there—
in that light. In that puddle.
Hearing voices:
"Why did you ever enlist?"
(Pause)
"Are you tight?
Is an asshole tighter than a pussy?"
That's what they want to know:
"Why don't you gag, when it's down your throat?
Are you always the woman? Or do you switch?"
Over and over and over:
"Why the hell do you like to suck dick?"

McGUINESS: We could give 'em the dog-joke:
"Why does a dog lick its balls?"

BILLY: *(Surprised by the "we")* "Because it can."

McGUINESS: And how can they argue with that?
So they stick us with lousy discharge papers:
so what? We'll be off of this ship.
We'll be alive.
I don't think there's a problem.

(BILLY thinks he's finally figured McGUINESS out.)

BILLY: You want to get busted.

McGUINESS: *(Agreeing)* Come here.

BILLY: And your buddies?

McGuiness: Fuck them if they can't take a joke.

Billy: Just leave 'em behind.

McGuiness: *Fuck* 'em.

(McGuiness's *coldness almost convinces* Billy *he's sincere.)*

McGuiness: Take your clothes off.

Billy: They say, "Strip."
Just so you know:
when they have *you* standing there,
in the light.

McGuiness: *(Nodding)* "Strip." *(Getting into it)* Faggot.

(At that moment, Hobie *wanders in—unseen at first by the others.)*

(He watches from the shadows, as Billy *starts to unbutton his shirt.* McGuiness *continues to play "Investigator".)*

McGuiness: Is an asshole tighter?

Billy: I don't know.

McGuiness: Is it hotter?
We *know* it's darker.

*(*Billy, *intent on undressing, doesn't answer.)*

McGuiness: Why do you like to suck dick?

Billy: Because I can.

McGuiness: Are you thinking about it now?
Or is that a banana in your pants?

(Out of a pocket, Billy *pulls the banana-peel he'd tucked away in Scene One. He tosses the peel aside.)*

Billy: No sir. I'm just glad to see you. *(By now, he's stripped to the waist.)*

McGuiness: Why?

Billy: Because I don't have to hide anymore.

(Pause)

McGUINESS: Why did you ever enlist?

BILLY: To be a man.

McGUINESS: But you aren't a man.

(As if accepting this judgment of himself at last, BILLY pulls off his T-shirt.)

(Now HOBIE can't take it, anymore—he steps forward.)

HOBIE: *(To BILLY)* What are you doing?

McGUINESS: *(Intense)* Beat it, Hobie.

(HOBIE grabs BILLY roughly.)

HOBIE: What the fuck are you doing?

(BILLY speaks, as if HOBIE were now the Interrogator.)

BILLY: Nobody could sleep below. That's all.
Hot night—two lonely guys—

HOBIE: You're lonely?
I was down there, too. Wide awake.
You could've—

BILLY: What?

HOBIE: *(Not sure himself)* I don't know.
I can smell you on my hands...

(BILLY pulls away. McGUINESS shoves HOBIE off to the side, to whisper.)

McGUINESS: Back off. I got orders, Hobie—
from the Captain.
He said, "Hey, I got an idea—
why don't you guys put on a show?"

(Before HOBIE can figure out what to do, DUANE enters, looking haunted.)

(CHOTKOWSKI follows him in, concerned. DUANE heads for the rail, away from McGUINESS, who's moving back to BILLY.)

(HOBIE, *adrift in the middle, moves to his buddies—but keeps a worried, possessive eye on* BILLY.)

CHOTKOWSKI: Duane? You O K? You were yelling.

DUANE: I had a bad dream.

CHOTKOWSKI: Wanta tell me about it?

(DUANE *stares out at the dark.*)

DUANE: (*Speaking of Japan*) What'll we see? When we see it?

HOBIE: (*Trying to reunite with his friends*) We aren't even close.

CHOTKOWSKI: Lotta miles and miles...

DUANE: (*Answering his own question*) Pagodas, right? Little bridges, cherry trees... In the dream, they were right out there... (*He points out at the dark.*)

HOBIE: Bull-shit. We're a thousand miles away.

(*Behind them—noticed only by* HOBIE—BILLY'*s moved up to* MCGUINESS, *putting his hand on the other's chest. He tries to unbutton* MCGUINESS' *shirt—but* MCGUINESS *firmly moves* BILLY'*s hand away.*)

(HOBIE, *unable to help himself, turns his back to the sea, and watches, as* BILLY *sinks to his knees in front of* MCGUINESS.)

(*Oblivious,* CHOTKOWSKI *tries to steady* DUANE.)

CHOTKOWSKI: Duane?

DUANE: What?

CHOTKOWSKI: Don't run.

DUANE: (*A whisper*) I want to go home.

CHOTKOWSKI: No shit. So do I.
That's why *I* ran.
In the valley. Remember?

(As CHOTKOWSKI *talks,* BILLY *nuzzles* MCGUINESS' *crotch with his head.*)

(MCGUINESS *makes a point of not responding—holding his arms at his side, not touching the sailor kneeling in front of him.*)

(*Dazed,* HOBIE *looks up and sees that* ALBERS *is coming onto the bridge.* ALBERS *stares down into the dark, trying to spot* MCGUINESS.)

CHOTKOWSKI: Now I can't sleep anymore.
I'm afraid of the things I can do.
All the terrible things.
Hold on.
A little longer.

(DE LUCCA—*worried about the captain—joins him on the bridge.*)

(*The moon comes out from behind a racing cloud.*)

CHOTKOWSKI: Anyway, the captain's off his nut.
Don't worry about the Mainland.
We are all gonna die a lot sooner than that.
ZIG-ZAG, YOU SON-OF-A-BITCH!

HOBIE: He can hear you.

CHOTKOWSKI: Who?

(HOBIE *points at* ALBERS, *on the bridge above them.*)

HOBIE: The Captain. Up on the bridge.

CHOTKOWSKI: Fuck him. (*He shouts.*) THE MOON'S COME OUT!
WE'RE SITTING DUCKS!

(*The moonlight also clearly reveals* MCGUINESS *and* BILLY, *about to have sex.*)

(*Astonished,* DE LUCCA *looks to* ALBERS *to act—but the Captain, grim, does nothing.*)

DE LUCCA: Sir?

(DUANE *sees* MCGUINESS *and* BILLY *and stares, not understanding.*)

DUANE: What is McGuiness—? Hobie—look.

HOBIE: No thanks.

DUANE: *(More urgent)* Chotkowski. What are they doing?

CHOTKOWSKI: Deserting.

DUANE: No, somebody *tell* me!

HOBIE: Escaping.

(At this moment, as BILLY *starts to unbutton* MCGUINESS' *fly, Captain* ALBERS *calls down from the bridge.)*

ALBERS: You there—on the deck! Would you move whatever it is you are up to—

MCGUINESS: *(Stepping back from* BILLY*)* A blow-job, sir.

ALBERS: —to the shadows under the gun?
Where I think you would have more privacy?

*(*MCGUINESS *isn't sure the Captain understands what's happening.)*

*(*HOBIE, DUANE *and* CHOTKOWSKI *uneasily watch.)*

MCGUINESS: THIS MAN IS A PERVERT, SIR!
UNDERMINING MORALE!
CREATING DISSENSION—

ALBERS: THEN GIVE HIM A VERY WIDE BERTH.

*(*MCGUINESS *is stunned.* BILLY *gets to his feet, knowing what he was afraid of, all along—that* MCGUINESS *was trying to set him up.)*

MCGUINESS: I DON'T THINK YOU UNDERSTAND:
HE WAS TRYING TO GIVE ME A BLOW-JOB! SIR!

ALBERS: YOU REMIND ME OF THE MAN WHO
COMPLAINS OF A FLY IN HIS SOUP. AND THE

WAITER REPLIES, "WOULD YOU KEEP IT DOWN?
OR *EVERYONE* WILL WANT ONE."

(While the other men are distracted by this shouting match,
BILLY *picks the stanchion up again.)*

(He approaches MCGUINESS, *hiding the metal bar behind his*
back, intending to kill his tormentor.)

MCGUINESS: THEY ALL *HAVE* ONE!
HE IS FUCKING EVERY MAN ON THIS SHIP!
FROM THE FO'C'SLE CLEAR TO THE TAFF-RAIL!
TRYING TO *FIND* SOMEBODY!
BUT WHERE IS HE LOOKING?
DOWN OUR THROATS?
THERE IS NO-ONE DOWN MY THROAT!
OR UP MY HEINDER!
WHY IS HE SEARCHING US THERE?

(Now DUANE *sees* BILLY *closing in on* MCGUINESS, *metal*
bar in hand.)

DUANE: *(Poking* CHOTKOWSKI*)* Jesus Christ—

CHOTKOWSKI: McGuiness! Watch your back!

*(*MCGUINESS *turns and sees* BILLY *raising his arm to conk*
him.)

(Startled, MCGUINESS *takes a step backward and slips on*
BILLY'*s discarded banana peel.)*

*(*MCGUINESS *takes a pratfall, landing with a bang on his*
ass. BILLY, *startled, lowers his club.)*

(For a moment, no one speaks or moves.)

(Then the craziness of the situation finally sinks in.)

CHOTKOWSKI: Saved by a fucking banana peel.

*(*CHOTKOWSKI *starts to laugh—and* HOBIE, *and finally*
DUANE, *join in, their laughter close to hysteria.)*

MCGUINESS: He was trying to kill me!
YOU THINK THIS IS FUNNY????

(This shuts the men up, for a second—then they burst out laughing again, even harder.)

(The laughter starts to die down.)

MCGUINESS: *(Staring, hurt, at* DUANE*)* Fuckit, Duane— even you?

(Abashed, DUANE *turns away—and sees something out in the water.)*

DUANE: What the hell is that?

*(*CHOTKOWSKI *turns to see what* DUANE *is pointing at.)*

*(*DUANE *is paralyzed with fear.)*

DUANE: It's fish...two fish...

CHOTKOWSKI: You've seen 'em before. And they always amaze you—

DUANE: No, *fish!* TORPEDOES!

ALBERS: *(On the bridge)* WHERE?

DUANE: Off the starboard—

(The ship is suddenly rocked by a huge explosion.)

(All the men still standing fall to the deck.)

(Another explosion)

(The lights change.)

Scene Twelve

(A small life raft—just a wooden ring with a bottom of wooden strips.)

(Mid-ocean)

(Lying in the raft, badly wounded, are HOBIE *and* DE LUCCA.*)*

*(*DE LUCCA's *right leg is broken;* HOBIE's *eyes are protected by a strip of cloth someone has tied around his head.)*

(Clinging to the sides of the raft—to avoid the punishing sun—are ALBERS, BILLY, CHOTKOWSKI *and* MCGUINESS, *who's looking around for* DUANE. DUANE *seems to be missing.)*

*(*DE LUCCA *and* ALBERS *are wearing life jackets. The rest are not.)*

(Since the night the ship sank, the men have been in the water for the following day and night.)

(Now they've come to the end of the second day—almost forty hours.)

(The men are weak, dehydrated, close to delirium.)

(Late afternoon. Still bright, but soon the light will begin to fade, very rapidly.)

MCGUINESS: I shouldn't have let him—DUANE!
Why the hell did I...

CHOTKOWSKI: Down the red lane.
Down the shark's red lane—

MCGUINESS: FUCK YOU! DUH-*WAYNE!*

HOBIE: *(For the umpteenth time)* I can't see.

ALBERS: It's the glare—off the water.

HOBIE: What glare? I don't see any glare—

MCGUINESS: FUCKING DUANE! YOU SON-OF-A-BITCH—...

ALBERS: *(To* HOBIE*)* It was driving you crazy, son.
So we had to blind fold you.

*(*HOBIE *touches his face and feels the blindfold; again, he's done this many times. He's confused.)*

HOBIE: Why?
What did I do?
I'm blind folded.
WHAT DID I DO?

(Suddenly DUANE *pops up from underwater, near* MCGUINESS.*)*

DUANE: It's there!

ALBERS: I don't think so.

(Furious with relief, MCGUINESS *reaches out and grabs onto* DUANE, *who isn't wearing a life jacket either.)*

MCGUINESS: You goddam goober.

*(*MCGUINESS *pulls* DUANE *back to the raft.)*

MCGUINESS: Stay fucking put.

CHOTKOWSKI: What's down there?

DE LUCCA: *(Emphatic)* Nothing.

DUANE: The ship!

CHOTKOWSKI: What ship?

DUANE: It's right below us!
(Pointing down:) See?
That's the top of the Number Two stack.
Right under our feet.

(Hearing DUANE *ranting,* DE LUCCA *tries to sit up in the raft. The effort makes him gasp.)*

ALBERS: *(To* DE LUCCA*)* Where the hell are you going, mister?

DE LUCCA: Trading places. *(Referring to* DUANE*)* You'd better get that man in the raft.

ALBERS: But your leg—

DE LUCCA: He keeps drinking sea water.

DUANE: *(Proudly)* Not now!

ALBERS: *(To* DE LUCCA*)* I can see all the way to the bone.
You can't put that leg—

DUANE: I don't have to drink sea water now.
It's fresh. Right out of the scuttle butt.
Cold as ice.
I drank `til I just about bust a gut.

HOBIE: (*Looking blindly around*) Where?

CHOTKOWSKI: (*Confused*) The ship didn't sink?

DUANE: Not all the way down.
Just a couple of feet.
Like it's waiting for us.
You just have to swim in
and you open a door...

CHOTKOWSKI: (*Trying to reason this out*) That'd flood it...

DE LUCCA: That's right. The man's gone.
Flying one wing low.
Get him into the raft.

DUANE: I'm THIRSTY!

MCGUINESS: (*Holding onto* DUANE) You think I'm not,
you bobbing turd?

HOBIE: I'm burning up.

ALBERS: The sun's well under the yard arm.
Wait it out.

HOBIE: But I have to get into the water.
Just to cool off.

ALBERS: You can't see.

BILLY: I can hold him.

MCGUINESS: I bet.

(HOBIE *blindly tries to clamber out of the raft.*)

CHOTKOWSKI: (*Out of the blue*) I can see an island.

(*Pause*)

HOBIE: Help me into the water. Somebody. Please.
I'm burning up.

(CHOTKOWSKI *and* BILLY *awkwardly help* HOBIE *over the side of the raft, and into the water. As they do so,* ALBERS *wriggles out of his own life jacket.)*

DE LUCCA: *(Almost crazy with pain, gritting his teeth)*
There has to be order.
Somewhere.
Why were we fighting?
Why did we go to war?
That man should be in the raft.

BILLY: *(To* HOBIE, *as he holds him in the water)* Better?

HOBIE: Than what?

(This cracks up CHOTKOWSKI *and* BILLY. *They laugh, a little crazily.)*

(The captain passes his life jacket over to BILLY.*)*

ALBERS: Get a jacket on this man. On the double.

*(BILLY *helps* HOBIE *get the life jacket on.)*

DE LUCCA: Captain. I think—if you won't wear a life preserver yourself, then get back in the raft.

ALBERS: When the sun has set.
My burns are already bad enough...

DE LUCCA: And when it gets dark?
Will you, quiet as a rat, let go of the side?
Splash...

(Pause)

ALBERS: I don't like you, Mister De Lucca.
I never have.

(Pause)

CHOTKOWSKI: I can see a goddam island.
There's a long white beach,
what looks like a valley above it...

McGUINESS: I thought you'd seen enough valleys.
You and me both, chicken shit.

CHOTKOWSKI: And this line of silver, must be a river,
falling down into the valley.
Can you see it?
Can anyone see it?

BILLY: No.

CHOTKOWSKI: If I could haul my raggedy ass that far...

ALBERS: *(Wanting* DE LUCCA's *life-jacket)* Mister De
Lucca—

DE LUCCA: *(Knowing what* ALBERS *wants)* No. Sir.
There is nothing out there.

DUANE: Lotta miles and miles...

DE LUCCA: Listen: if there was a shore,
we could hear the surf.
This steady roar...

ALBERS: But he needs to go.

DUANE: *(To* CHOTKOWSKI*)* You said don't run.

CHOTKOWSKI: I ain't running.
If I could get help...
Save one of you pitiful bastards...
I *swear* I can see a beach.

DUANE: All the terrible things you can do...

CHOTKOWSKI: And palm trees. Tall ones...
Shifting in the breeze.

DUANE: All the terrible things...
(Pause)
Remember how that valley felt?
Like the mouth of an animal.
I looked around, and—
everyone was gone.

(Pause)

MCGUINESS: I WENT BACK FOR YOU!
(Pause)

Chotkowski said, "Fuck him.
He's a piece of dead meat.
Lying there
with his cock in his throat.
Let him lie."

(Pause)

DUANE: It's all right.
The reason I didn't run—
I was so scared shitless—
down my leg, I mean, shit—
how *could* I run?

CHOTKOWSKI: Don't *forgive* me, you son of an apple-
knocker.

DUANE: I'm not—

CHOTKOWSKI: I said DON'T FORGIVE ME!

ALBERS: *(Offering* CHOTKOWSKI *permission) Is* that surf?

DE LUCCA: I'm not giving this man my jacket.

ALBERS: You are if I—

DE LUCCA: No. I'm relieving you of your command.
Sir.

(Pause)

ALBERS: I will see you in hell.

DE LUCCA: If you let us die, I believe you will.
You knew the moon had made us a target.
What did you say? You said, "Good".
I HEARD YOU.
"Good."

(With the other men distracted by this fight, CHOTKOWSKI
starts to swim away.)

DE LUCCA: *(To* ALBERS*)* Let go of the side.
If that's what you want.
Rat-bastard. Splash.

You don't give one rusty fuck for the men
in your charge.
You don't give a fuck about anything.
Only your son.
And your son is dead.

(Pause)

DUANE: *(To* ALBERS*)* Does he look like you?

ALBERS: No. Handsome. At least a head taller.

DUANE: I saw him.

ALBERS: What?

DUANE: He's on the ship.
Right below us. Chug-a-lugging champagne.
With a beautiful woman—

DE LUCCA: Shut up.

DUANE: A blonde. With legs up to here.
Is that his wife?

DE LUCCA: Gyrene, that's an order—SHUT UP!

(In his agitation, DE LUCCA *jars his broken leg and screams in pain. No one moves to help him.)*

DUANE: Like Veronica Lake, a little?
Except in a family way?

*(*CHOTKOWSKI *is far away from the life raft now.)*

(At last he disappears.)

ALBERS: My son is dead.
And my ship is on the bottom.
Miles below us.
Please be still.
The sun is almost down.
You can climb back into the raft,
for the night—

DUANE: But I'm THIRSTY NOW!

ALBERS: All of us are.

MCGUINESS: *(Shaking* DUANE*)* Did I tell you not to
drink salt-water?
Did I?
"Bonk...bonk...bonk...bonk..."

DUANE: *(Looking down)* I think they're dancing.
(Looking closer) Making love?
No, dancing.
Can you hear—I can't hear the music...

(Pause. BILLY *starts to sing.)*

BILLY: "Down in the jungle lived a maid,
of royal blood though dusky shade..."

DE LUCCA: Tell the invert to button it, would you?
Also tell the invert he's on report.
I saw the advances he made.
When they pick us up—

HOBIE: NOBODY IS PICKING US UP!
WE LOST OUR POWER BEFORE THE SHIP COULD
SEND OUT AN S-O-S!

ALBERS: You don't know that.

HOBIE: Ask my wife. We are all gonna die.
(Pause)
Where is Chotkowski?

(Pause. The others finally realize CHOTKOWSKI *is gone.)*

BILLY: He went to get help.

HOBIE: There is no help. CHOTKOWSKI!
(Pause)
Can you see him?

MCGUINESS: Hard to look that way. He must be
swimming right   into the sun.

HOBIE: Is the sun that low?

*(*HOBIE *takes the blindfold off, but still can't see.)*

DUANE: They've started turning on the lights.
Down there.
See that watery glow?
This handsome man and this beautiful woman...
dancing on the bridge—

ALBERS: MY SON IS DEAD! *(He starts to cry.)*

HOBIE: Somebody is crying...

BILLY: The captain.

DE LUCCA: He isn't the captain.
(Pause)
There has to be order.
Or why did we fight?

(The light begins to fade more rapidly, now.)

DUANE: *(Looking down)* Wait a minute—
that's *my* girl!
On the dancefloor...wrapping all of her
legs around his—...
I *told* you she was a whore.

DE LUCCA: You said you were, too.

(Pause)

DUANE: I'm thirsty.

(Pause. DUANE suddenly pulls away from MCGUINESS.)

(He dives beneath the surface, disappearing.)

MCGUINESS: DUANE!

DE LUCCA: Let him go.

MCGUINESS: Fuck you, buddy. DUANE! Oh Jesus,
Duane...
I was holding on, this time,
I was holding ON!

DE LUCCA: He was out of his mind.
And he wanted to die.

Do you want him to kill *two* men?
Let him go.

McGUINESS: I WON'T! *(He swims away from the raft.)*

(Frantically McGUINESS *searches for* DUANE.*)*

(But DUANE *is gone, and* McGUINESS *himself is exhausted.)*

(He starts to go under.)

(BILLY—who's been holding HOBIE *up in the water—moves* HOBIE *up to the raft.)*

BILLY: *(To* HOBIE*)* Hold on to the raft. Can you do that?

HOBIE: Where are you—no. Don't leave me.

BILLY: Your buddy's in trouble.

HOBIE: Don't leave me!

(BILLY kicks away from the raft to rescue McGUINESS.*)*

(DE LUCCA reaches out a hand and grabs HOBIE.*)*

DE LUCCA: I've got you, O K?

HOBIE: Tell my wife she was right to stop sending me letters.
She knew.
Tell her—

DE LUCCA: Tell her yourself. You aren't dying.

HOBIE: Tell her women know everything.

ALBERS: *(More to himself than the others, starting to lose it)*
My wife said good-bye to us both. At the station.
My son and I.
She held onto me long enough to whisper:
"Bring him back".
That was all she would say to me.
"That's an order, Mister. Bring him back."

(At this moment, BILLY *reaches* McGUINESS.*)*

(He grabs the marine by the neck of his T-shirt, starting to drag him back to the raft.)

(McGuiness struggles feebly.)

McGuiness: Let go of me, you faggot—
Duane! Let me GO! I HAD him!

Albers: Every mother's son...

McGuiness: —by the hair...
DUANE!
But he started to slip away...

Albers: "Bring him back."

McGuiness: ...through my hand...

(Billy has pulled McGuiness back to the raft.)

Billy: *(To De Lucca)* Can you help me?

Hobie: *(Calling out to Billy)* Where are you?

Billy: *(To Hobie, as De Lucca lets go)* Hold on till we get this man in the raft.

(De Lucca—grunting with pain—grabs hold of McGuiness, weakly pulling him in as Billy—in the water—pushes.)

(Finally McGuiness flops onto the bottom of the raft, gasping and coughing up water.)

(Billy now grabs hold of Hobie again, holding him up.)

Hobie: Hey sailor...

(Hobie clings to Billy.)

(For a moment, everyone is still—from shock or exhaustion.)

(Billy holds onto the raft and buoys up Hobie.)

(Hobie floats, held up by Billy's arm.)

(McGuiness, coughing less, is trying to catch his breath.)

(De Lucca grits his teeth, riding out a wave of pain in his broken leg.)

*(*ALBERS *bobs in the water, holding onto the raft and watching the other men.)*

*(Then—quietly and deliberately—*ALBERS *lets go of the side of the raft.)*

(He sinks into the water, disappears. No one sees him go.)

(With great tenderness, BILLY *kisses* HOBIE—*his face, his hair, his neck—as* HOBIE *dangles in his grasp.)*

*(*McGUINESS, *hearing something, stirs.)*

McGUINESS: Hobie...

BILLY: He's dead. *(He continues to kiss the lifeless body.)*

DE LUCCA: Then let him go. Save your strength.
LET HIM GO!

*(*BILLY *ignores him.)*

(Offstage, the men who drowned begin to make the sound of breakers on a shore: "poosh...poosh...")

McGUINESS: Listen...

DE LUCCA: What is it? *(He scans the horizon, terrified.)*
What *is* it?

BILLY: Why are you so afraid?

McGUINESS: I think it's surf...

*(*BILLY, *still in the water, holds onto* HOBIE, *tighter.)*

*(*McGUINESS *and* DE LUCCA *strain to sit up in the raft. They look out at the swelling dark.)*

DE LUCCA: Waves on a fucking beach.
We are not gonna make it.
All of us are insane.

(The sound of surf fades out.)

(The light, very rapidly fading, suddenly swoops to almost black.)

McGUINESS: No.
I can hear it too.
I *think* I can...
I can hear the shore...

(*As* McGUINESS *and* DE LUCCA *wonder if rescue is possible,* BILLY *starts to kiss* HOBIE's *body again, in a fury.*)

(*The dim light fades—in a second—to black.*)

END OF PLAY